# Connoisseurs of Worms

"What a strange, profound, and beautiful book this is, with its insistence on pursuing precisely that whose nature it is to elude pursuit! The widening range of Warren's restless attention encompasses aesthetics, the arts, nature, the difficulties of perception, and the complicated psychic dynamics of aging; and she tackles all of it in language that bristles with intellect and passion, discipline, and a yearning to break free. How irresistible I find her invitation to join in her pursuit, in poem after poem in this dazzling collection."

—**Rhina P. Espaillat** on *Dream with Flowers and Bowl of Fruit*

"Ms. Warren's poems combine imagination with intelligence, music with emotional energy. The language sparkles in poem after poem."

—**Dana Gioia** on *Zero Meridian*

"Warren is among the very finest American poets who still observe the strictures of meter and rhyme. She informs her work with lively feeling, wit, wisdom, and memorable music; she keeps us sitting up and interested."

—**X. J. Kennedy** on *Zero Meridian*

DEBORAH WARREN

# Connoisseurs
## *of*
# WORMS

PAUL DRY BOOKS
*Philadelphia  2021*

First Paul Dry Books Edition, 2021

Paul Dry Books, Inc.
Philadelphia, Pennsylvania
www.pauldrybooks.com

Frontispiece by Grant Silverstein

ISBN 978-1-58988-156-3

Printed in the United States of America

Library of Congress Control Number: 2021934257

# Acknowledgments

Poems in this book have appeared in the following publications:

*Able Muse, Angle, Arion, The Classical Outlook, Commonweal, Dogwood, Dramatic Monologues: A Contemporary Anthology, First Things, The Hopkins Review, The Hudson Review, The Larcom Review, Literary Matters, Mezzo Cammin, The Sewanee Review, Think, The Warwick Review, The Yale Review*

# Contents

# PART I

## *Connoisseurs of Worms*

# Mole

Earth is his occupation, and the mole
works the turf in his native breaststroke, swimming
hallways into the sod—a geonaut
supreme, and connoisseur of worms; I've heard him
breaking roots an inch beneath my sole
and seen how the subterranean specialist
carves out for himself a single, simple role.

I envy the expertise he brings to bear
on dirt, the narrow office he was given;
as for me, my habitat is thought,
where I grope and sweat and scrabble out a living
forced to prove—up here in a windy lair
as invisible as the mole's—that there exists
an animal who can dig a hole in air.

## In Extremis

Lucky possum who, caught in a crisis,
      doesn't have to do a thing but yield:
A stroke of narcolepsy takes control,
and stunned by an automatic anesthetic,
his body seizes up. The sudden coma—
      the silver corpse dead to the wood and field—
is unfeigned out-and-out paralysis,

and it keeps the howling, yipping things at bay
      by telling the world: *nolo contendere.*
*Playing* possum?—as if it were a role
and he a gray marsupial Juliet?
*Acting?* No. He's sleeping out the drama
where, making of "death" a sanctuary,
      he lies until the trauma trots away.

## Un bar aux Folies Bergère (Manet)

I'd like to describe an accident I had
where I fell suddenly into two dimensions.
I was standing at the kitchen table
thinking about my winter jacket, maybe,
maybe about the Black Death, or the dog;
my arms isosceles to the table's surface,
hands, on both sides, out along its edge—
I'm someone else! a trick of recognition,
and in a flash my body is transposed

into the barmaid *aux Folies Bergère.*
I'm there. I've been assumed into the picture
where I've taken flesh among the bottles,
hands on the marble bar, and in the mirrors
the chandelier, the smoky room, *buveurs*;
the velvet ribbon around my throat, the locket;
and under the rose in my décolletage,
I'm corseted into a serious hourglass.
There'll be heartburn before the night is out.

It's a painting. It's flat. Pick at the surface;
no way in—there's no z-axis. But
I'm there, in Paris, 1880-something.
And now I fold my arms, widen my stance:
I'm Mr. Clean. A couple of cushions: I'm
*Maja desnuda.* I'm the Discus-thrower.
I'm Christina yearning across the field.
I just pick up the pose and run with it
like Proteus escaping from himself.

## A Sunday Afternoon on the Island
## of La Grande Jatte

Seurat atomized an afternoon
where bright dots infinitesimal
fuse into a summer Sunday,
sun, shade, water, parasol.

Keep your distance. On close examination
any grand design turns into small
bodies bobbing loose in space—
beings that don't have any point at all.

# Alboin and the Princess Rosamund

Pavia, 565–573

Alboin killed the Gepid king
and took the daughter for a wife.
Their marriage was like any other:
he had issues—lying, brawling,
grassy teeth; she would have loved
to have it formally annulled.

It wasn't for philandering
that Rosamund finally took his life;
it wasn't his stink; she wasn't bothered
by his abuse of alcohol;
what galled her was his habit of
drinking from her father's skull.

# The House Oblique to the Road

For half a mile the houses face the street,
façades square in their rectangles of lawn,
except one: Turned at thirty-odd degrees,
it slopes off—paused—poised in mid-retreat
as if it's at the edge of moving on
and, shoulder to the road it never faces,
glances sidelong down its granite sill
as vertigo throws all its vertices
one minute in, one minute out of stasis,
unequal to the strain of standing still.

# C. elegans

*Caenorhabditis elegans:* genome sequenced

Groundbreaking news about the nematode
*C. elegans*—an even simpler beast
than they had thought, with a genetic code
nineteen percent identical to yeast.

And now I hear that the sequencing machines
associate me with *him*—with *vermin*—by
festooning us in matching strands of genes:
A common heritage I can't deny;

but a worm—he's less than dirt, the über-low
doormat to the world, bred to submit
and never turn (except earth-clods), and so
unprepossessing. Except I've also read

how it's supposedly the meek who hit
the jackpot—the big legacy—and earn
what great *H. sapiens* inherited:
the earth that *elegans* was first to turn.

# I.D.

The Titian-haired orangutans
loop the trees or, shoulders rolling,
forage—palm to sole, palm to sole—
    the Sumatran forest floors.

Each has a fingerprint (like man's,
the loops and whorls uniquely his)
and, no matter how distinct it is,
    very much like yours.

## Euglena

In the diaphanous *euglena*
emeralds—beads of chlorophyll—
float against the plasma wall
delimiting its single cell:
However peppy its flagellum,
however fluidly it sculls
(flailing across the pond), it's scum,
neither plant nor animal.

On bristle-parapods the lugworm
mines the ocean floor and moves
an inch of sand.

    The placoderm
fins around the lake—improves
enough to bubble—ooze—slither—
waddle up the bank and tread
the fern.

    The frog's gills sag and wither.
Then a tree rat, quadruped,
promotes itself to chimpanzee,
swings down and walks on the savannah—
finally equipped to see
its own beginning as *euglena*.

# PART II

*Churning Pixels*

# Gelomancy

*divination based on the interpretation of laughter*

The world, in the pressure of creation—
atoms at its core colliding—
shook with their reverberations,
shuddered its surface into fissures,
  split its sides, and laughed.
And where the laughter left a grotto,
crouches a hag who drinks the sulfide
  in a volcanic draft.

To the interpreters she utters
truth: The sulphur-priestess squats
  and, sucking from the earth
its cold upseeping exhalations,
babbles her intoxication
burped out into cachinnations—
croons and chuckles up the future—
  oracles of mirth.

# The Olive Eaters

The man had ordered wine, and the waiter
brought them a plate of olives and some bread.
Across the two-foot square of damask table
there was a universe that went unsaid.

Apparently the terrible expanse
deterred them both from crossing it: He ate,
and, faced with the complicated damask flowers,
she fixed her eyes on the mute blue olive-plate.

# PETscan

*D'où venons-nous? Que sommes-nous? Où allons-nous?*

The radiologist's technician
fondles visually (in gamma rays)
the piece of me they'll be evaluating
on a positron emission scan.
He does love his big machine—
which lacks some capabilities:
It can't
zoom in on such elemental quanta
that, in the churning pixels, I could see
(inside myself, and in high definition)
electrons boinging and clinching on the screen.

It lacks a gear for retro-vision:
Atoms, rushing into the early me,
would show up, coupling and agglomerating,
snapping together the instant I began.
It lacks a setting further back,
to where each atom was before they mated.

But then, if there's a forward gear to track
the particles, sick of me, going their separate ways,
dial it back—as I disintegrate—
to its benign low-resolution haze.

# PART III
## *On Stage*

# Theatre Lobby

In front of us in the queue, a woman wearing
a tiger print. From neck to wrist to ankle,
it clings to her billowing arms and dimpled buttocks;
lobes of soft flesh overhang her knees—
better imagine her into something else:

*From the Sumatran forest, or Bengal,*
*or out of the Ganges mangrove-swamp, a tigress*
*tall on her hind legs, reaches the head of the line.*
*Behind her, all around her in the foyer,*
*conversations merge in a background roar.*

The usher, pink with awe and acne,
*studies her ticket—but his lowered eyes*
*swivel upward over the marbled fur*
*flowing across her shoulder and flank, the muscles*
*in low relief under the chandeliers.*

And now her black and ochre body
*gleams and with its shifting pattern*
*brings into the heated lobby*
*an uneasy little stir.*
*Threads of envy eddy through the crowd.*

# I, vi

> This castle hath a pleasant seat; the air
> Nimbly and sweetly recommends itself
> Unto our gentle senses.

Duncan and Banquo, trotting in,
halt to admire the castle's site,
the tender air where nesting martins
ride the dusk before alighting
five stories up under the battlements.

Hautboys, torches, barking, shouting
herald the entry of the king;
the pock-jawed groom comes grinning out;
such amenities, and making
such a good impression on the senses:

summer, nestlings—and the croaking raven
already fledged out in the spreading dark:
Drop the curtain; leave them there—believing,
witless, and eternally arriving
among the pretty deer in the castle park.

## Swan Lake

Up from the lake in a liquid pirouette,
splashing satin and tulle in a spray of prisms,
the white swan, radiant, floats on the radiant air.

The black swan follows—an *S* of polished jet:
Small iridescences shift and flicker where
the black plumes and a blacker magnetism
make Odile more dazzling than Odette.

## Sleeping Beauty

A hiker stumbled into a sudden clearing—
panting and briar-raked, swung down his pack,
and stopped on a paved walk under a château where,
between the geometric flowerbeds,
an antique woman—slippers, scrambled hair,
collapsed lips—clawed the stones with a balding broom:
Stripping off his shirt, the young man stood
a moment to wait for his lungs and legs to mend.

She watched him drink, his white throat cambered back,
the spilling water glistening down his breast.
Her eyes hung pink and low—she shuffled nearer,
patted her wilted bodice, wagged her head,
screwed her glance at the stone façade gone threadbare,
and gummed and tongued a tale of a turret room:
That's where I spin the cold days into years,
she said; I doze and wait for a *special friend*

(the parterres winked) to arouse my maidenhood
as fresh as these young roses; all my resting
kept my body young, my face intact:
a hundred years and now a happy ending.
And the garden—triangle, circle, *demi-lune*—
didn't blink as, through the boxwood squares,
he backed away to the trail he'd bruised through the wood
and fled down into the aging afternoon.

# Revolution

Out of his diaphragm the ventriloquist
throws his voice to a little mannequin
who catches it in his clapping mandible,
responding exactly as his master says.
But one day the dummy finds a way to fumble:
Pumped too full of windy vocables,
he unsags—swells up—he's about to go
some kind of crazy: I'll just step away.

He's going verbal—verbal like a pistol.
The plastic jaw is softening into skin;
he molds himself a lip, tongue, palate, muscles,
smiles around the corner of his face,
rolls the smile back in to a small pink circle
and spits a blast of shrapnel—plosives, glossals,
fricatives. This guy packs some audio
but, like his owner, has little to say.

# *English 152:* Daydream

Sanders Theatre, Cambridge

Sanders Theatre. Harry Levin's on stage—
a fifty-minute lecture on a play.
Today it's *Timon of Athens*. But today
    the protagonist is a fly:

it's busy in the Gothic window panes,
where its relentless *basso continuo*
(drowning out the professor) steals the show . . .
    and hums a lullaby . . .

. . . Timon . . . Greece . . . the first Olympic games,
the flies who, lest they plague the celebrants,
departed from the venue in advance—
    just before opening night,

or so they say. Back then, flies knew their place,
*out* of the amphitheatre: courteous,
they stayed on the far bank of the Alpheus
    till after the closing rite.

# Priority

The earthquake woke Caruso. Plaster fell,
the chandelier bounced demented on its chain,
The vertebrae jumped on his spine, wainscoting cracked—
 *but did his voice still work?* His spirits swayed.

And when they evacuated the hotel,
the door-frames shuddering, Caruso stayed
and ran through a suite of scales to ascertain
 that his tenor had survived the shock intact.

# Abul-Abbas

Baghdad's caliph, Harun al-Rashid,
presented Charlemagne with Abul-Abbas
to keep as a personal pet. You could ask, What
would a Frankish emperor want with an elephant?
An extra paladin?
        No, but Abul-Abbas
joined his master in the northern wars
to rout the raider Godofrid the Dane—
to win back Friesland, flat, flooded (and rich).

You would be wrong to label Abul-Abbas
matériel, or an animal aide-de-camp.
He went as a companion to Charlemagne,
who wouldn't travel without him—furrowed, leaden,
prized over any North Sea tidal plain.

Call him impedimenta or attendant,
When Abul-Abbas died at the chilly Rhine
the emperor called an end to the campaign.

# PART IV

## *Limbless Psyches Slogging up the Cumulus*

# Common Cause

When Solomon was born, birds came soaring,
waddling, swimming, flapping around the air.
They cheeped and honked to celebrate the day;
a few chipped in to give him a layette—
eiderdown, eggs, and less-appetizing things.

*Ad hoc* solidarity to honor
David's gilt- and purple-bundled heir:
canary, pterosaur, and cassowary,
hummingbirds flanked by penguins fishily sweating;
everyone who could fly (or not) was there.

They waited—jostled—shoved at the nursery door—
brawled, guano flying, everywhere
blood, owl pellets, drifts of white duvet,
gamboge splots of yolk on the baby's blanket.
All they had in common was their wings.

# Vashti's Tail

Vashti refused to dance for Ahasuerus
naked, as he wished; even the timbrels
stuttered to a halt, embarrassed.
Vashti's reason? It was simple—
horror at cavorting bare;
a reason so absurdly tame
that rumor whispered secret pimples,
boils or, better, leprosy,
or worse: how fabulous if Vashti
had, and hid—as gossip claimed—
something too awful to unveil
coiled against her coccyx, where
they said she bore a spotted tail.

# Psychopomp

Hermes, the Valkyries, Saint Michael—
    the big faiths feature various
pilots for the disembodied soul;
        they blaze the trail for limbless psyches
        slogging up the cumulus
or mark the channel through the Stygian shoals.

Nice idea, and dead wrong. Nothing divine
        (Hamlet's mistaken) shapes our ends,
which means, instead of the choice of two or three
exotic destinations, I'm resigned
to the local Woodlawn, where I'll spend
        my personal eternity.

True, there's a certain tedium to a tomb.
I could be spirited off by Allah's guide,
flown into Barzakh, that dim purgatory
(a layover en route to a happy doom
staffed by hot girls—maybe my own houri).
So many ways to be taken for a ride.

# The Gopher-Wood

And Noah heard Him—all the specs:
the thirty cubits, triple decks,
the gopher-wood God had in mind,
the very vessel He assigned—
he'd build it. But, before he could,
he'd have to get the gopher-wood.

Lumber: It requires trees.
To fit so many refugees
in something that could be immersed,
he'd have to plant a forest first.
And any woodsman knows you can't
just go get gopher seeds—and plant.

You have to cultivate the ground
before you scatter seeds around.
Then you can watch the seeds beginning
germinating. Then there's thinning,
which will give you (no time soon)
saplings big enough to prune . . .

And after all that, you can just relax
a hundred years, until you need an ax
to fell the fat bright timber. Hire a smith,
when the planks are sawn, for the nails to join them with.
Then—when you're finished, that's when you begin.
Take the nails and hammer the first one in.

# The Translation of the House of Loreto

(Saturnino Gatti, 1463–1518),
Metropolitan Museum of Art

In 1291 the Virgin's house at Nazareth was miraculously
transported by angels to escape the victorious Muslim armies . . .
it came to rest at Loreto, on the Adriatic coast of Italy.

Look at the picture. Totally insane.
A house ups from the earth and comes to rest
intact as a virgin—a continent away.

You bet it takes a miracle to explain,
and of all the ones I've heard this is the best:
a pair of angels shows up to convey

a building, on their fingertips. Okay,
shifting a house a couple of countries west,
I know one thing you *can* be sure about,

a job like this, you're looking at a crane.
No wonder they found it cheapest and easiest
to hire a couple of angels to carry it out.

# Rebekah's Ultrasound

Jacob and Esau struggled in the womb
right from the start. Rebekah's ultrasound,
quite early on, revealed the embryos:
two fat big-headed commas—yin and yang,
grappled together head to toe;
Rebekah only eleven weeks along,
they were duking it out in there already.

The sonogram was the usual fuzzy mess.
Chaos roiled the screen; the babies
sent the amniotic waters heaving.
If this were a satellite feed, we'd see
the Doppler radar of a cyclone forming,
But the forecast couldn't tell Rebekah
whether Jacob or Esau was coming first.

# Christening in Andover

Mary Monica won't remember
the trickle over the fontanelles,
the daub of oil: what sticks is the name.
Soon the fluid bones will close;
give her twenty years—she (still the same

Mary Monica) won't resemble
this small froth of lace and gauze;
men will daub her with their eyes,
and this same flesh will have hardened
into someone else when the varnish dries.

# PART V

## *Bêtises*

# Zebras, Morning

The moon drips down the damp tree, running thin
across the black grass; soon the same tree combs
morning down through its branches: ray by ray,
on the yellow grass the strips of long sun slide
between acacia tree and acacia tree,
and the zebras stretch and shake night into day.

The zebra himself is black, at least his skin;
but an ancestral freak in the melanin
veined the hair with white. The anomaly
moved the impressionable chromosomes,
and now the stripes on his coat have settled in,
permanently pouring down his sides.

The zebra rarely gives himself away—
effacing himself in the shade. But I imagine
something the black and white of his surface hides:
a shock of color where a harlequin—
his heart—is playing crowded hippodromes,
tumbling an ancient red-blue comedy.

# Utilitarian

Take your Helios, Ra, or Roi Soleil,
god and monarch crowned in sun,
flashing gold around their glossy thrones.
    Glory's very nice;

but take Apollo, laureate of light:
Flamboyant boy! Phoebus (i.e.
a being sculpted out of lucency)
    is also the Prince of Mice:

he routs the pests from herds and granaries.
Do we really need a god to represent
music and poetry? And what's prophecy
compared to an art like rodent management?

# Down-to-Earth

The coyote yip-yip-yips: imminent danger;
    the dog in the kitchen rumbles a basso growl;
the field sends back a shrill elastic baying;
    the kitchen gives a soprano howl.

These two aren't discussing climate change,
    war, flu, layoffs; in this dialogue
a well-informed coyote's not relaying
    to a pessimistic dog

grounds for worry—national cases of mange,
    the mountain lion population swelling,
a cougar-sighting fifteen miles away—
    only a future close enough to smell.

## Ex Nihilo

Stitch a rooster to a snake;
cover the seam where they're attached:
you've produced a cockatrice.

Gather some simple mermaid parts—
girl, glitter, Lycra, caudal fin;
polish the items, mix and match,
and soak them overnight in brine.

Go celestial. Glue together
light-years of lumens, a man, and feathers,
and call your angel-hominin
God's agent—a six-pinioned seraph.

Assemble a harpy à la carte:
she won't be difficult to make;
collect the components—just combine
a woman's body, bird-claws, wings.

A satyr: get a goat to graft
onto a man—a half and a half
spliced in a hairy synthesis.

Or aim for pride and grandeur; craft
a gryphon—insignia of kings,
by crossing an eagle with a lion.

These are easy, mongrel things.
You take what you've already got—
with pre-existing pieces draft
a hybrid; it's a snap to patch
one part to another.
                      But
if even the pieces don't exist?

A project you create from scratch?
Even before you can begin,
you won't begin, since there's a catch:

It's not the materials. It's your mind—
intelligent enough, but not
capable of the freak of thought
that conjures up an animal where
all you have is empty air.

# Three Snails Argent

On the family coat of arms three silver snails
in single file on a sable field
glide in place under the winged crest. Time

stopped them dead. On imaginary slime
the gray whorls move across the shield
leaving behind no glittering silver trails.

# The Gyascutus

—an imaginary beast

The Gyascutus grazes the steep terrain—
the acme of adaptability:
his left (uphill) legs shorter than the right
      at the angle of the slope.

Slow, loplegged, he circles the mountain, always
counterclockwise—a hoofed and hungry planet;
spiraling widdershins around a hill,
      he noses the alpine vetches—

up and down the scarp in a one-way orbit.
Pausing on a high fell, he looks out
past his muzzle, downward, down to where
      a flat bright pasture stretches

horizontal—and he drops his head
and carries on over the crags and hillocks
like an absurd ungulate allegory
      representing Hope.

# Quarry

Minos prayed for a bull. Poseidon listened,
sending him a foam-white animal
as incandescent as moonlight in a sea-mist.
Then his queen seduced it—and bore a monster.
All Crete shuddered, disgusted. And all Athens
trembled. What a disaster.
                                    Still, the fact is,
that freak cowchild was just a foolish mooncalf,
grazing on pebbles and stone dust: It was Minos
who commissioned the hungry beast's quaint pasture;
it was Minos who fed him Athenian children.

Icarus bullied him. And Ariadne
teased him and chased him with snorts and dusty laughter
between the high walls, hurling gravel at him
until he ran—his ankles tangled in strange threads—
white-eyed with terror, from dead end to dead end.

# The Eumenides (Kindly Ones)

If Purgatory sounds bad, try the snakes
Orestes faced. Just let the Furies find you—
scalps curling with serpents. And they're worse;
not mere wigged-out constrictresses: their curse
works on the soul. Their tresses hiss behind you;
their own special pressure is to squeeze
transgressors into madness. No one shakes
the just scales of the Mistresses of Sin.

Whipping offenders into penitents,
they operate the same on everyone.
I hear that if even the Titan Sun
strays from his path, they're there to drive him in
in time for his morning shift—and if you take
"drive" in a neighborly carpool kind of sense,
or think that post-Orestes they got kind, you
flatter them. They're no Eumenides.

# The First Naiad

> with sea-cocktails and incantations, Naïs
> turned her lingering lovers into fish. (Ovid)

One night with a lover was enough:
let him loiter, knocking at her door
a second evening?—her gray eyes would grow
ultramarine and shrewd. She'd give him wine
poured from a murex shell into a glass,
and to the purple liquid she would add
seawater thick with ocean-dust. The lover,
heated now with Naïs's charms, drank deep.

Soon his arms, stretched out to seize her, stopped,
fell to his sides and hugged his ribs—and stuck;
his fingers merged and thinned to a frill, his feet
fused into a fringe: the former lover
writhed and glistened between new pulsing fins.
Weary, bored by the process, Naïs (noting
the final accordion fever of his gills
scorched in the shrill sun) braided her weed-long hair
and practiced her scales and the songs that worked the wine.

She sang, and her song stirred up the drops of plankton.
But, regrettably, on her tides of tunes,
reports of her fish-charm finally floated out.
One of her lovers slipped a Mickey Finn
between the indigo stanzas of her salt spells—
and there was no more music. The notes slid down
to pool at her feet, and a pleated silver skirt
sprang from her ankles, thrashing the sand. A cyclone
spilled her into a river, where she swims
goldfish-bright, like fire under the water.

# Mosquito in the Heart

*There's nothing visible on the EKG.*
So says the cardiologist.
Wrong. Clearly he missed
some small anomaly:

With an incessant and insistent hiss
under my left ribs—a falsetto whine,
whetting its proboscis,
it flits and ricochets around my heart.

The doctor's diagnosis?
He'd call it a feint of heart—if he had the wit:
He doesn't. He's content just to be smart,
and here's his opinion: *It's anxiety.*
*It isn't in your heart—it's in your mind.*
*There's medication; often meditation*
*helps with tension.* And he won't admit
that coronary insects do exist.

Just paranoia? I'm not buying it:
He'll give me white lies but—when I insist—
refer me to Cardioentomology.

# Lycanthrope

I'd say the werewolf is a lucky guy.
He gets to read the moon and memorize it,
howl out the lunar text in fluent lupine,
and when the lyrics pall and the moon grows old,
he reverses himself—but reserves his second self,
leaving his fur in a spot at the edge of the wood.

His latent talent's a two-sided coin—
except that, heads or tails, both sides are downsides:
the werewolf enterprise is either/or,
where neither option wins the day (or night).

Observe the electron. One way or the other,
however you look, it has it all together,
a particle and a wave concurrently
without the trauma of toggling between the two.
The werewolf, though, has no integrity.
He's less than one, or worse—he's two times neither.

At noon it's warm, but soon the sun grows cold;
and later his alter ego claws at him—
an itch in his skin for a pelt and yellow eyes.

## Cephalopoda sepiidae

It's all about color with the cuttlefish.
His triple heart pounds the blue-green blood
in emerald tides through vein and artery.
He's not a fish: he's Proteus in the flesh,
mimic—impressionist. And this is true:

As an embryo, he'd watched through his jelly wall,
itching to hatch. When his yolk was getting old,
already he'd combed the currents, tracking prey.
Out of the egg, he hit the water hunting:
he's all palate. Gemmed in chromatophores,

in bright cold blood he beats the coral coverts.
Variety artist—polyp, anemone;
sapphire, silver, nonpareil—
he flees at a shadow: with a plume of ink,
        he's nothing but a stroke of sepia.

# Identify the Following:

Mary of Exeter:
(a) eight-fingered abbess of Saint Morwenna's Convent
(b) pigeon deployed in intel and special ops
(c) "Cancer Filly," racehorse tinted pink
(d) clairvoyant toddler, daughter of King Canute
(e) transvestite thief: the "Hanesville Robin Hood"
(f) a varietal rose named after a prostitute
(g) creator of edible wigs.
The answer: She
received The Dickin Medal for Animal Valor
(1945), for *devotion to duty*
and *conspicuous gallantry*, conferred
on *Mary of the National Pigeon Service.*
Flying cross-Channel missions, Mary endured
shrapnel-wounds, a hawk attack, a bomb,
a wingtip severed by gunshot—undeterred.

I hear them in the eaves, fouling the gutters,
murmuring in their throats encoded words,
monotones in pidgin Morse—but is
this bobbing, feathered thing a noble bird?

# Reveille, 11:00 p.m.

> I am . . . a companion to owls
> Job 30:29

Owl, in spite of your reputation
as an icon of sagacity,
Job, comparing himself to you, referred
not to wisdom but to desolation.

Poor Job. He was a poster child for pain.
Whenever he felt particularly forsaken,
God said *Deal with it*. And being screwed,
naturally Job tended to complain.

Let's forget about Job. Up, owl! These woods,
your library and laboratory—lonely
and as sweet as red to a hummingbird—
they're what I hunger for: Job was mistaken.

Owl, shadow in a violet shadow, wake up.
In the scurrying field, in the star-freckled sky,
open the night and read its adumbrations.
I want you alone for company.

## Pons Asinorum

*bridge of asses* (*Elements*, Euclid, Book I, Prop. V)

This is the bridge that stops the speeding
scholar—where the easy thoroughfare
narrows over a little river, where
the textbook takes the quick beginner, leading
him along and then, *right here*, impeding
any further progress: In despair
at more complexity than he can bear,
he balks. Beyond this point there's no proceeding.

The water purls, however, right below
the bank and, on a bank so pinkly flecked
with clover high in the water-meadow grasses,
the scholar can let the rest of Euclid go,
saying he's had enough of intellect,
and stay here on the near side with the asses.

# Water Tiger

Lord of the pond, the predacious diving beetle
      surfaces to seize a supply of air;
he lifts his wings, secures a silver bubble,
      and drops to his offices underwater, where
he liquefies his prey with jets of spittle,
      sucking the local salamanders dry
until the evening—when the inexorable
      water tiger takes to the August sky.

Flying up from the pickerel-weed and beating
      the drops from his wings, he whirrs aloft and eats
the evening air. In the dark he sets his sights
      on some new promising pond, where the moon's reflection,
betraying water below him, winks and beckons—
      and sizzles to death in a roadside electric light.

# PART VI

*Calibrating Infinity*

# Gladys and the Exploding Baby

She didn't mind watching's Krista's Henry,
Gladys said. So Friday night, at seven?
Krista, with her husband in the service—
    Krista, twenty-two years old—
had to go out sometimes after all.
    Krista always tried to pay her;
    oh—no, Gladys always said,
    I couldn't; Henry's good as gold.

Gladys arrived. Henry, in pajamas,
kissed his perfumed mother and at eight
(nine-thirty), after stories and milk, preferred,
    shrilly, not to go to bed:
Henry's forehead rumpled—then the shirred skin
    filled, the creases pressed up flush;
    his eyes bloomed out as blue as grapes;
    his veins stood up and percolated.

Gladys patted her heart. The situation:
Gladys fluttering, Henry swelling and red—
(a flash of sciatica daggered Gladys's hip)
    purple—oversaturated
violet—indigo—cyan; Henry steaming,
    Gladys bleating, Henry boiling,
    Gladys retreating behind the door.
    Krista wafting home too late.

# Intersection

A girl pulled up in the lane beside me,
smiling, in a luminous private sphere,
playing across her lips some scrap of thought—
a joke on the radio, a memory,
some plan or fantasy—and passed
inches away, her profile perfectly clear,
but sealed inside a membrane of safety glass,
and every inch between our cars a light year,
her invisible itinerary
one moment tangent to my own, and caught
glancing off into another galaxy.

# Boy Stung by a Bee

Two astonished seconds follow the dart
    into the ankle punctured by
        a barb of melittin—

but he knows motion better than he knows bees:
    He pricks the air with treble cries,
        jerks his foot from the grass,

throws back his head, hugs his knee to his heart,
    and hops mad circles to exorcise
        the venom stuck in the skin.

Don't tell him that in a minute the sting will pass;
    if you want a unit of time he'll recognize,
        you'll have to calibrate infinity.

# Pressure

Put a little pressure and heat on rock,
give it time, and shale turns into slate.
It's the same with calcium carbonate
slowly reinventing itself as chalk.

Limestone's in no hurry; it started to harden
during the Lower Jurassic into marble.
Graphite spends millennia on diamond:
The luxury of eons.
                    At any rate,
slow or slower, they move in mineral time
with plenty of leisure for maturing late.
Nice for them. I have a different clock,
skin-shallow. Animals can't afford to wait.

# Anonymous Valentine

Sending a card to a guy I barely know
comes on strong, even for a valentine:
Why let you know I'm thinking about you? So
     I'm sending it unsigned.

You can make up a woman, when you get it.
Don't put February in her bones.
Give her a body younger (and a little
     better) than my own.

Fabricate, for the faceless girl who sent it,
skin, eyes, hair. And—if I do confess
the card's from *me* (not the figure you've invented),
     and you're unimpressed,

you can keep the hot exotic who
     came on like a holiday
in the heart of winter. She's ideal for you,
if, that is, she ever comes your way.

# Equivocal

The fire leaked between the logs and splashed
up in a hissing spray, and drops of flame
showered down and dried on the hearth;
through the coals the red heat purled and trickled;
cinders bubbled and melted into ash.
And if I listened enough the fire became
the rain, and both of them were both—
the water-sparks that popped in the spout outside
and the fire that rippled up the chimney: liquid,
single-minded, and unsatisfied.

# The Scourge of God

Attila, sacking Aquileia, drove
the Aquileians east before him
      into a swamp that later bore
watery Venice on its back,
      shored up by what had been canals of gore.

Attila—tattoo-cheeked Kazakh—
died of nosebleed; now palazzi
      float where he howled with his Hunnish brutes, before
axe and sword and savagery
      ceded to civilized techniques of war.

## Cupressus

The cypress thrusts a black stiletto
up through the rumor of cicadas,
swallows the radiance out of noon
and allows the ground a foot or two of shade.

Sleep there, and the roots will surface,
pierce your brains and suck them out—
that's what the goatherds say. I wonder
what the cypress would want with human thoughts.

I have thoughts enough to spare;
the heavy monotone vibrato
frets and simmers in the heat;
and I'll lie here and rest for an hour or so.

# Lady Mondegreen

> mondegreen, *noun*: a misheard song lyric

"They slew the Earl of Moray
    *and laid him on the green.*"
Those last five syllables (misheard)
buried the fatal blade again
    in *Lady Mondegreen.*

Up, up out of the mossy sward
    she sprang from the hot red blood
shed by a slaughtered Scottish thane:
a nonexistent lady on
    a nonexistent bier.

She left her misbegotten name—
    a by-blow of the ear,
a slip of the dirk—she who had been
nobody and who even as
    she came to life was slain.

Hunt from Ross to Dumfriesshire;
    you'll find no corpse to bury
matching the bonny wraith that was
the brief and brave phenomenon
    of Lady Mondegreen.

# Ellen Bright

—dream (November, 2009)

Before I quite woke up, she flitted in—
not much more than her name; but in a dream
a cameo appearance is enough,
and I saw everything I needed to know.
    The main thing was that Ellen had come to stay:

the type who takes the dead lamp and rewires it
gets around to seeing Mary Jo
(the hospice visit I've been blowing off),
knows how to work the idiot TV,
    also the jumper cables, makes sorbet—

Ellen was here. She was someone I'd admire.
We'd complement each other, as a team.
Maybe we wouldn't actually be friends—
she'd be too busy. And it occurs to me
    how much I would dislike her anyway.

# Tough

    The Spartan boy who steals a fox
hides it and endures the roiling mound
        scratching at his proud breast under his tunic,
its claws hooked in his skin. He keeps
        his slashed neck veiled beneath an impassive mien.
The shoppers chatter past without a clue.
        It thrashes and tears into his flesh in panic.

    He weaves among the helots and hawkers.
Its canines engrave his ribs. He lurches around
        the Lacedaemonian ladies in the street.
The longer and closer he keeps it, the deeper
        the secret gets its teeth into his veins.
He crumples. The rusty beast springs into view
        and out of the town on even redder feet.

# The Toughness of Grace Crackbone

b.1565, Great Yeldham, Essex

A graft by marriage onto the family tree,
Grace may have brought some good genes to the breed;
but when I have my genome done, they'll find
(rummaging around in the pairs of bases)
none of her gentle Christian name in me.
The surname suggests a second trait of Grace's—
but even if I descend from Crackbone seed,
neither is strength an attribute of mine.

# 360°

All afternoon the wind complained, and the willows
would have come to blows—but yielded
(being willows), swimming along the air.
Thick with purposes, the same wind—squealing,
rocketing down my narrow veins,
      taking the corners fast—

spun out into a hurricane in my heart
and made of my will a weather-vane:
      Reading every gust,

it shifts at the wind's direction and, too willing,
hoarse on its hinges, bats in vain
      and croaks and spins, not getting anywhere.

# Human

Sucking strength from the fertile earth, Antaeus,
butcher, roofs his cave with travelers' bones;
      but if his clod-feet leave the ground,
his thick force drains back down into the stones.

Hermes, however—lightwalker, ascending,
pilot of souls, succor of wayfarers—
      kicks his sandals, spurs the wind,
climbs the sky and runs across the air.

And if—born like Antaeus from the dirt—
I soak up that same giant chthonic thrust,
      I'm Hermes too, and at six feet,
I like to forget my name itself is dust.

# Climbing Etna

We'd see the lava, nights, from the town square,
as if the sun—an egg of fire—broke
at dusk, threading its incandescent yolk
down a mountain hanging in black air.
Every night we'd scan the dark horizon
looking for those streaks, and every night
they took a while to find, however bright:
Etna, it seemed, had spent the evening rising
off the earth, to hover even higher,
as if the mountain meant not to be found.

And then, today, we ran the flows to ground,
climbing up to the rolling burns of fire—
closer, into the shimmering air and hiss
that glanced up from the thick and red-flecked river
—until our soles were smoking. But the lava
sang, inside the mountain: *Come, discover
the fire's origin and genesis;*

*more—the heart of the world, in its enceinte
of blind white heat.* Seeing the lava course
wasn't enough, or watching the rock decant
the sun. What brought us up here was the force—
the hot loins—of a lightning god as dark
as thunder; and, like Eve, like Semele,
we wanted to approach. But there's a spark,
a jewel older than geology:
stop shy of it—of finding the fire's source,
of closing in on what you shouldn't see.

# Perspective

The time is six a.m.—uncivilized,
but it can take an hour getting through
the rudiments too indispensable
to skip, like morning shower and shampoo.

Offer soap to the Neanderthal
scraping a hand-axe out of brittle bone,
his matted body crusty with sores and flies?
What he wants is a decent piece of stone.

# Hydrographic

The rain scribbles its way into a brook,
the river scrawls itself into the sea,
the waves inscribe their cursive on the shore:
Water's as legible as any book.

And when the fog erases the ocean air,
a fog-eye reads into the vacancy
lines ghost-written in the motes and more
intelligible for not being there.

# Closer

Like a muffled metronome
behind me, there are footsteps walking—
much too close. I cross the street,
because it must be me they're stalking.
But the cadence of the feet
in iambs on the dim concrete
comes closer, closes in, repeats
in my ribs: my own heart knocking
and outrunning me—a clock,
its hands quicker than feet. It's beating
time, a tuneless shadow locked
inside me, where I hear its omen
sure-footed and close to home.

## Peaceable Kingdom

Edward Hicks, 1833

Wolf and lion and lamb (and children) pose,
well-behaved. It's a picture of a field trip.
Still, can oil-on-canvas keep them this way,
side by side and amenable, much longer?
Paint what you want to—but what optimism
brings together a pasture and a forest?

# PART VII

## *Readout*

# Readout

The nurses watch the sets of blinking numbers,
each gauge with its particular high and low—
respiration rate, oxygen flow,
blood pressure, temperature, the EKG
graphing the heart's dynamics, rhythm, tempo.

But wheel the monitors away before
the digits pulse the patient's way to zero.
Shift your gaze to him, and let him blur
in a continuum, in a legato
so smooth the nurses at the bedside see

his passage as a slow diminuendo:
Let him vanish by degrees;
let the dying body fade and go
transparent; finally there will be
only the nurses around an empty bed.

## Memento Mori

Being thin, I feel mortality
more than most, because it's always there
in rib and hipbone, right beneath my skin.
Here in my wrist and clavicle I see
my skeleton laid prematurely bare—
the frame under the flesh. Because I'm thin,
my sternum, sacrum, and my stony spine,
at night especially, rise up to remind
me I'm a living ossuary. Yet,
haunted by my bones' gaunt pokes and fey
elbowings, I'm glad enough to let
them prod me with their message—*Seize the day
with metacarpals wide*—not to forget
what waits only a thin membrane away.

# Late Mowing

A clanking took me out in mid-July
to watch the mowing—so delayed
the farmer said, "The good hay's over;
it's all fescue now." I asked him why
he mowed the hay at all if late hay paid
so poorly—June's alfalfa, clover,
timothy and bluegrass sell for feed,
but this? He was practically throwing his time away.
"Money is money. I could go
to an early grave, with this year's debt; I need
to live, and—mulch or feed—all hay
is the color of money. That's why mow."

Money is money, green or gold. Pretend
you're the hay, though: Color matters, in the end.

There's death and death, just as there's hay and hay.
And when he comes, I'll make of him
a scarlet tractor trailing a scythe
like this one, green as June's blue grass. I'll say,
Daylight-reaper, don't be grim.
Mow this hay and lay it to dry
with light's whole spectrum of machinery,
windrows swept with a yellow side-rake
clanking. Come with just this tune—
and after the clover and the timothy;
wait, like this, for mulch hay; make
it very late, way after June.

Red tedder, orange baler and wagon—this way,
come like a kind of carnival for hay.